breathe!

don't give up
on your dreams!

have
courage!

be content!

drink plenty of water
and get exercise!

support
each other!

laugh
often!

smile!

embrace
serendipity!

Oh good!
Before you read this book,
I have something important to tell you . . .
You're wonderful, amazing,
and, above all else, you matter.
Happy smiling!

Andrews McMeel Publishing
a division of Andrews McMeel Universal
1130 Walnut Street, Kansas City, Missouri 64106

www.andrewsmcmeel.com

20 21 22 23 24 SDB 10 9 8 7 6 5 4 3 2 1

ISBN: 978-1-5248-5829-2

Library of Congress Control Number: 2020937422

Editor: Patty Rice
Art Director: Sierra S. Stanton
Production Editor: Margaret Daniels
Production Manager: Tamara Haus

ATTENTION: SCHOOLS AND BUSINESSES

Andrews McMeel books are available at quantity discounts with bulk purchase for educational, business, or sales promotional use. For information, please e-mail the Andrews McMeel Publishing Special Sales Department: specialsales@amuniversal.com.

Disclaimer: Smiles are contagious and can spread happiness . . . so smile often!

Everyday Smiles

Finding joy in every moment

And, suddenly, my day is better.

hug hug

smile smile

A 4amShower Comic Journal

Guy Kopsombut

Andrews McMeel
PUBLISHING®

This page left intentionally
blank for your imagination.

For my mom, dad, sister,
and anyone needing a smile.

I'm a big fan of smiles. Like a big one. To the point that I believe that a single smile can change the world. Sometimes a single smile is all that's needed to turn your world around. With enough smiles, I think we can change THE world.

To help us along this journey, I've written this book to help you smile every day. You might be thinking, "Every day? But some days are just so hard. There's no way you can smile every day!" Oh, but I think you can! You may find a smile from a partner, friend, or sitcom show. But my favorite place to discover that smile is within yourself.

Over the years, I've built up a chest of positive thoughts that I refer to whenever I'm feeling down. No matter how hard times get, I can find a smile in my inner reservoir. This is not to say that I don't experience sadness, anger, or any other emotion. That wouldn't be healthy. What these smiles allow me to do is stay on track in my life and know that whatever is thrown at me, it is never the end of the world.

So, this book will help you generate your own compendium of joy. Whenever you are feeling down, you can come back and remind yourself what brings a smile to your face.

Take your time going through the book. No need to rush! As you go through it, remember to take time to reflect and breathe. Things will be ok :)

Thanks for smiling with me,

Guy

Ready to smile? Let's start!

Oh! Just one more thing before we start . . . I am a big fan of serendipity and discovery. Throughout this book, I've hidden little bits of joy to help you smile. For instance, there is a heart on every single page in this book. Can you find them?

(Here's one!)

Take time **to** self-reflect.

Welcome **to the** beginning **of the** book.
Beginnings **are** happy **places.**
Things are fresh **and** new **and the** possibilities **are** endless.
I find that beginnings **are the** perfect place **to reflect.**
So, let's make **this** page your happy **place.**

List/Doodle/Paint ALL **the** things **that** make you smile.
They can be big **or** small **or something** in between.
(I've listed a few of my own just in case you need help.**)**

Puppies   Dinosaurs wearing   Getting hugs
                                funny hats

Those make me smile, too!

You **can** always **come back and** add more **as you go** through **this** book.

This is the compliments-only page.
Who are the compliments for, you ask?
For yourself, silly!
It's easy to be overly critical of ourselves
and forget what makes us wonderful.
Jot down all the great things about yourself here—
no matter how big or small!
(I've started you off with a few.)

I have a wonderful smile.

I recommend the best TV shows and books.

Go on! No need to be bashful! Gush away!

Whenever you're feeling down, come back to this page to remind yourself of all the wonderful things about yourself.

Sometimes . . .

. . . the best
conversations
you have . . .

. . . are the ones
you have
with yourself.

Love yourself.

You always make **my** days better.

When things go wrong, we all react differently.
Some get angry, some get sad.
Since reactions come naturally, it can be hard to control them.
What we can control is how we react to our reactions.
Take a moment and answer these questions.

Who do I want to be?

How do I want to react when things go bad?

In the heat of the moment,
what can I do to remind
myself of who I want to be?

Better? Better!

Think of someone you love.
What are some of their best traits and characteristics?

The next time you see them, compliment them!

I love your thoughts and ideas!
You're doing a great job
filling in this book!

I think **I** love you.

Let's share **a scoop of** love.

Do you feel like you're in a creative rut?
Whenever I'm stuck and can't think of ideas,
I let my mind wander and create a world of its own.
I give myself permission to be silly and allow the impossible to be true.

Why not give it a try? Reimagine the following items with a twist!

A shoe

A tophat

A cat

A cup

A computer

A tree

I love sprinkles!

9

Think **of** someone you care **about.** How can **you** sweeten **up** their day?

♥ **Small things**

 Medium **things**

♥ Big **things**

Oo, they'll love all of those!

You are **my** sweetheart.

It's ok to ask for help.

Having a bad day?

Here's a sure-fire way to brighten up your day: help brighten up someone else's!
You'll find that when you do, their happiness will spread to you, too!
When you're having a hard time, though,
it can be hard to think of positive thoughts.
So let's plan ahead!

List the people, organizations, and groups that matter to you.

What makes them smile?

Cookies!

Now, when you're feeling down, you have a list of concrete things
you can do to change your mood!

Your home is more **than** your **physical shelter.**
It's a place that you feel safe **and** secure **and** happy.

Draw/Doodle/Write **out what makes** you feel at home **below:**

What makes you feel safe **and** secure?

What makes you feel loved?

What makes you feel happy?

What makes your home unique **to** you?

You are my **home.**

Work hard, **but** remember **to** take breaks!

Work-life balance can be one of the hardest things to achieve.

What are the goals that you are trying to achieve?

Why do you want to achieve them?

Who are the people you care about?

How are your goals affecting these people?

* stroll
stroll*

Some days, it's not easy to smile.
There may be turmoil inside of you that you feel like no one can relate with.
I find that on those days, the best thing to do is to write
down your feelings.
While this won't instantly solve your problems, it can help you reflect
and see life from different perspectives.

Take a moment and write your troubles down.
When you're able to solve them, come back and cross your troubles out.

Tada!

Sometimes the world falls apart.

But, luckily, you are there to pick up the pieces.

And help put it back together again.

All is not **lost.**

Your voice is music to my ears.

Like smiles, music has a way of changing our moods.
The type of music we listen to can determine how we feel.
Let's make a playlist for the next time you need a smile.

What songs always bring a smile to your face?

What songs fill your heart with joy?

What songs bring happy memories to your mind?

What songs get you dancing?

*strum
strum*

Let's have **a** dance party!

Draw **out the** steps **to** your **own** original dance **below!**
(Using stick figures is fine**!)**

I love
your moves!

Put on the playlist you created **on the previous page and** try **out** your dance!

"Let us read,

and let
us dance;

these two
amusements
will never
do any harm
to the world."

-Voltaire

What a
wonderful day.

Let's enjoy the simple joys in life.

Ugh. I can't think of any ideas.

This is the worst.

I'm the worst.

I won't be able to succeed.

This won't do.

This is the worst.

I'm the worst.

I won't be able to succeed.

clear clear

There. Space for ideas.

Don't limit your possibilities.

Are you stuck in a loop of negative emotions?
A way to get out of this rut is to be kinder to ourselves.

In the left column, write down your own self-judgments.
In the right column, write what you would
say to a friend who said those things to you.
How would you cheer and encourage them on?

Self-judgment   Encouragement

Remember to
love yourself.

Welcome to the reassurance page (sibling of the compliments-only page).
Read the following out loud as many times as you need to.

I am beautiful. I am wonderful.

I am loved. I can love.

I can think. I can dream.

I can heal. I can forgive.

I am capable of growth.

I can sing. I can laugh. I can dance.

I can learn. I can create. I can overcome.

I can make a difference. I can do good.

I am compassionate. I am empathic.

I can work. I can rest.

I can reach my dreams.

I can breathe.

Breathe.

I can smile.

I matter. ♥

_____

(Sign your name here)

Your smile can change the world.

You can help the world.

The world is a big place and it can seem daunting to help.
But if we break down the world into smaller parts,
things become more manageable.

What causes mean the most to you?

What are things you can do to help . . .

• Daily/Personally (Small changes matter!) . . .

• Locally . . .

• Globally . . .

Thanks for the help!

Of course!

If you find yourself getting overwhelmed, take a break
and reflect on the good you have done.

We live **in a very fast-paced world.**
Take a moment **to** clear your mind **and**
"just be.**"**
Reflect **on** your experience. **How did it** feel**?**

*meditate
meditate*

Life can be a puzzle.

Sometimes, it might feel like the pieces aren't all there.

But you're smart, clever, and capable.

And you'll figure it out.

You **can** overcome **your** challenges.

Let's do nothing **together.**

Oh no! It's raining outside.
Let's have **a stay-at-**home day.

Doodle/write your perfect **indoor** day below.
What items do you **need to get** comfy?
What activities will you **do? What are** your snacks?

What a fun day!

Some days, it can feel like we're not making any kind of progress at all.
On those days, it's good to reflect on yourself and where you're going.

Let's take a second to plan out your life.

What are your long-term goals?

What are your medium-term goals?

What are your short-term goals?

Now let's work backward.
Draw lines connecting your short-, medium-, and long-term goals together.

I find that when I'm feeling lost,
seeing how my goals connect together
reaffirms that I'm on the right track.

If you feel you're not, plan out your goals again!

Making your bed.

clean clean

Exercising.

jog jog

Reading a book.

read read

Some say small wins don't matter.

flip flip

Done!

But the small wins give us confidence for the bigger ones.

So don't forget the low-hanging fruit.

You can succeed.

You will find yourself . . .

. . . when you get lost in a good book.

Self-discovery **is only a** chapter away.

Books **are** amazing **things.** They can **take** us **to** worlds far **and** beyond.
They can make **us into** heroes **and** provide **a** safe **space.**

Who is your favorite character **from** your favorite **book?**

Wow! That's my favorite
character, too!

What makes you like **them?**

What can you do **to** replicate **those** characteristics?

Life is more fun when you're playing co-op!
Think of someone you care for deeply.

What are their favorite foods?

What do they love doing?

What makes them smile?

What are their favorite songs?

Now, plan a special day **just for** them!

What a great plan!

They'll love it!

Let's always play co-op.

Any day is **a** good **day** if it's with you.

When things go wrong in my life,
I try to reflect on the things that matter the most to me.
By doing so, I can put my life into perspective.

List five things that matter to you.

What are a few ways you can show gratitude?

Without rain,
we wouldn't have flowers,
so I guess rain isn't
all that bad after all!

Have you ever felt like your creativity is being restricted?
Maybe it's because of self-doubt or fear of criticism.
Over the years, I've discovered that
when those feelings arise, it's a sign to go ahead and try.
I find that I sleep better at night when I'm honest with myself.

Draw yourself being creative in your favorite way.

You brighten **my day.**

You make **me** feel like **a winner.**

With so much social media in our lives,
you may find yourself seeking the approval of others
and end up doubting yourself in the process.

Rather than impress others,
what can you do to impress yourself?

I love how this
turned out!

Switch your mindset
from jealous to inspired!

Sometimes our needs and wants get jumbled up together
and it becomes hard to choose how we live our lives.

List out all your needs and wants below.
(I've included a few of the basics for you.)

Eating fresh foods
Exercise
Sleep

Reflect on what you need to concentrate on now and what can come later.
Now, put each into a column.

Now   Later

A key step in reaching
your goals is prioritizing!

All we need is **each** other.

You'll always look great **to me.**

People often worry about their appearances,
but I find that nothing warms people up to you more than a friendly smile.

Write down your favorite jokes here.

Who in your life might need an emotional band-aid right now?

What are some things you could do to help their healing?

You help make things better.

You fulfill **my** life.

What are the things that keep you energized?

Find time **each** day to do **at least one of these things.**

Oh hey! You're halfway through the book!
Let's take a breather.
(Both in reading and in life)

Before we do,
it can be hard to pause if we have a million things going through our minds.
Why not take a second to unpack everything to clear your mind?

Below is a box. It's a box of thoughts.
Add whatever is on your mind into it.
Bigs things, small things, this box can hold it all!

It's quite a lovely box.

Box
of
Thoughts

Ready to relax? Let's go!

Step 1: Breathe in deeply

Step 2: Breathe out deeply

Step 3: Breathe in deeply

Step 4: Breathe out deeply

(You're doing great)

Step 5: Breathe in deeply

Step 6: Breathe out deeply

Step 7: Repeat 1 to 6 as needed!

Feel free to refer back to this guide whenever you need it!

If you find your mind wandering, it's ok!
Acknowledge the thoughts and put them in the box.
Then focus on breathing again!

Box
of
Thoughts

(You can now get your things from the box.
Or, maybe take only a few items.
The box can hold things for a very long time.
You don't have to hold it all on your own.)

It's an underwater sea party **and** everyone **is** invited!

Draw **in your** favorite critters **below!**

Fold the page toward you at the dotted line, one section at a time.

Fold the page backward at the dotted line, one section at a time.

And here?

Yep!
I love you in the air,
sea, and in between.
Our love has no bounds.
Let's join the party below!

... my favorite place
will always be
beside you.

... high or low ...

Here?

*splash
splash*

Yep!
Get ready
to swim!

No matter if we go
up or down ...

Here?

Yep!
Let's dive!

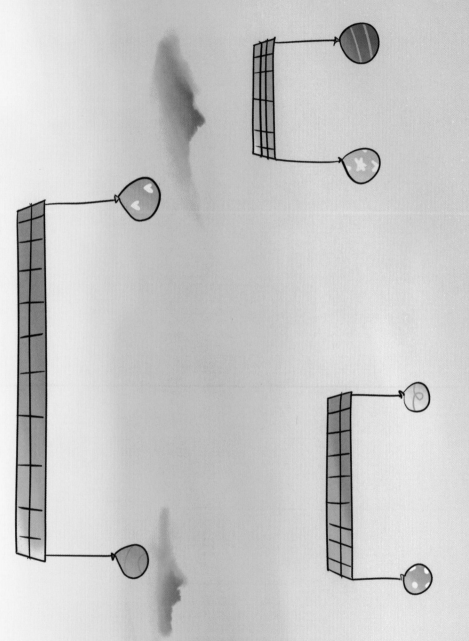

What a lovely sunset!
Draw **the animals** enjoying **the** hot-air balloon festival.

Life presents us with many choices and
it can be hard to know what to do.
Having a life motto can help steer you toward the right path
and remind you of what you stand for.
Let's create one!

What are your principles?

What matters to you most in life?

Now, create a short phrase that culminates these ideas.
Try to make it short and catchy so you can remember it!

Mine is
"Do good. Think big.
Work hard. Be great!"

Live **a** purposeful life.

Our love transcends all **boundaries.**

When was the last time you sat down and just colored?
Take a moment to relax and fill in this picture however you like.
(Feel free to color outside the lines. In fact, I encourage you to do so!)

When was the last time you let your
imagination go wild?
Draw the silliest, most unbelievable creatures below.

You're very impressive.

The world can be
mean and awful.

But you're a
part of this world.

*dig
dig*

And you can
take a stand.

*whoosh
whoosh*

You can make
a difference.

You can be **the** change.

As we hustle through our day, it's easy to take for granted what allows us to live, like clean water and fresh food.

Take a moment and list/doodle a few life necessities that you are grateful to have.

Routines make us more efficient,
but they can make us lose out on some of the wonder in our world.
In order to take the horse blinders off, write down your daily schedule below.

Below are a few ways to welcome serendipity into our lives.

-Take a walk
- Read a book
-Go to the museum
-Doodle
-People-watch
-Listen to music

Add a few into your schedule above!

Moving forward
can be exhausting.

You see your goal
in sight . . .

. . . But also
the journey ahead.

In times like this,
take your eyes off the prize.

And look forward
while enjoying the view.

This moment is yours.

Today, **I'll** make time for you.

We often rush through our days wanting to do the best for our loved ones. But, by doing so, we can end up putting those very loved ones on the sidelines. Let's take a moment and cherish those who mean most to us.

Draw a portrait of someone you care about here.

Blast off!

hop hop

When was the last time you shared a moment with them?
How do they fit within the schedule on the previous page?

Sometimes those who seem most cheerful can be hurting the most.
Take time to reach out to your friends and see how they are.
Even if you don't have answers, merely listening to someone can make
a world of difference.

Let's practice our listening. Go outside and listen to the world for 20 minutes.
Do not speak or write or do anything else other than listen.

Done? Write down what you heard both within and outside of yourself.

*rustle
rustle*

I'm here for you.

You **don't have to** face life **alone.**

Life can be a scary thing, but by overcoming your fears,
you can be the hero in your own book.
Each hardship you overcome becomes a part of your legend.

Let's try visualizing who we will become.
First, what is causing you distress, fear, or stress?

Write out a courageous tale in which you overcome these hardships.
Feel free to use your imagination.

Wow! What a hero!
Can I be your sidekick?

Going through a big life change can be quite overwhelming.
We all have the ability, though, to help others who are struggling to smile.
What are your favorite ways to encourage someone you care about?

Simply listening to someone in pain
can make a world of difference!

Now, look in the mirror and encourage yourself!

I support your transition.

You help **me** be **a** better person.

Have you ever found yourself losing control?
If you do, take a moment to look around and
take inventory of all the wonderful marvels surrounding you.

Focus on one particular object and appreciate it.
Now, look up to the sky. Whether it's blue, filled with stars, or full of rain,
appreciate that you and it exist.

What are the little things in your life that bring you joy?

You are my island in the sun.

Losing someone
you love is
never easy.

But if you remember
the good times,
they'll always remain
in your heart.

Hold their love close **to you.**

Some days are just plain hard.
These are the days where we might have to let someone go,
either emotionally or physically.
On these days, know that it's ok to be sad. It's ok to be angry.
It's ok to grieve. It's ok to feel the emotions you are feeling.

When you're ready, think back to the good times you had with them.

What made you guys laugh?

What made you guys smile?

Take a moment to thank them within your heart
for helping you grow and become the person you are now.

The world can be a turbulent place
and your footing may feel unstable.

Fill in the rocks below with what keeps you grounded.
These are the things that, regardless of change,
remind you of who you are.

I'll always look out for you.

It takes a village to fix the world.

There are days where it seems like the world is ending.
Everything goes wrong and the odds are stacked against you.
These are the moments that will define you.
These are the moments in which you can take a stand and be a leader.
Don't give up! Answer these questions to re-energize yourself.

What makes your cause worthwhile?

Who are the people you will help by succeeding,
both directly and indirectly?

How can you approach your problem empathically?

Let's think
things through!

What are the consequences for failure?
Will those consequences matter in a year? Five? Ten?

I believe smiles can help **make the** world **a** better place.
What can you **do to** help **someone** smile **on a** daily **basis?**

You are loved. Pass it on.

I believe in you.

Welcome **to the** mythical tea party!

Draw **each** mythical creature below.

Unicorn   Dragon   Bigfoot

Feel free to invite **anyone else** you **would like.**

You're **not** alone **in this** world.
There are **people who** care **about** you.
Take a moment **to** reflect **on all the people**
who have been kind **to** you **over the years.**

Jot them down here.

How have they been kind **to** you?

Remember to
always say
"thank you!"

Let them know **how much they mean to** you.

If you're in pain, please reach out. You're not alone.

I want **to** smile with you.

Everyone **has lonely** days. Know **that this loneliness is not forever.**
Until **things** change, **take** time **to** better **yourself.**
When you meet someone **to** talk with, **you'll have more things to** share.

How **do you want to** improve **yourself?**

How **do you want to** grow **as a** person**?**

What **are some** activities you **can do to** improve**?**

Reading is a great way
to improve yourself!
It expands both your
mind and perspective!

Life can feel empty from time to time.
There are different ways to fill our lives with joys, though.
The key is choosing things that complete our lives rather than hurt it.
In Japanese culture, there is a concept called "Ikigai."
Ikigai means "a reason for being."

Fill in the Ikigai chart below.

Life is fulfilling **with** you in it.

Life couldn't get **any** better.

Whenever I feel down, I like to put life in perspective.
A few impossible things had to occur for us to exist.

- The Earth had to have formed within a habitable zone!

- The Earth was able to develop life because it is perfectly positioned between the other planets.

- Asteroids tend to hit the other planets with strong gravitational pull!

- The Earth had to contain a solvent to support the creation of life. That solvent is water.

- Because that solvent is water, the Earth has the benefit of greenhouse warming.

- The Earth is the perfect size to contain our atmosphere.

Against all odds, we exist.
What would you like to do with the time you have to experience life itself?

We are made of star stuff!

When was the last time you stargazed?
Draw your own constellations.

A shooting
star!

Make a
wish!

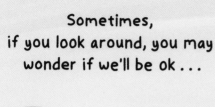

Sometimes,
if you look around, you may
wonder if we'll be ok...

...with all our nationalities
and differences.

Look further,
beyond the horizon.
Expand your perspective
and you will see...

...that we're not so
different, you and I.
That we're all connected
amongst the stars.

We're all stardust.

I'll always have love for you.

Think **of** someone you love **or** like-like.
Write their name **in the** hearts.
For each heart, think **of** why **you** like them.

Have you ever wondered what the meaning of life is?
Well, since everybody has a different life,
it stands to reason that life will have multiple meanings.
Let's define yours!

What do you care about?

Who do you care about?

What do you **love to** do?

What do you **want** your legacy **to** be?

Mine is to help
you smile.

Love who you are.

It's easy to get jealous in our social media-driven world.

What skill!

That jealousy can turn into sadness.

What do I have?

Know that you're more than your "likes" and follower count.

breathe breathe

You can shine bright, too!

So pretty!

I like you.

Technology has enabled us to buy most things online.
But some things can't be bought.
What are three things that make you happy
and don't cost a thing?

1.

2.

3.

Why do these things make you happy?

Did you know you're the hero of your own story?
Things may be rough now, but your tale isn't over yet!
Write your story below from start to end.

Once upon a time...

And they lived happily ever after.

Show **the** world **who is boss.**

You're **my** everything **and** more.

Think of someone you really care about.
What are the moments you cherish the most with them?
Write them down below!

What fantastic
memories!

Keep making more memories until the entire page is filled!

Hey. You're amazing, **you know that?**
You've gotten this far in life, **and that's fantastic.**
Plan a day **for yourself** below and pick a date **to do it.**

Morning

Afternoon

Night

Let's do all those things!

I want to be wowed with you.

You may turn your back on the world . . .

*boop
boop*

*dig
dig*

. . . But I won't turn
mine on you.

I'll be there for you.

Life can be lonely, but you are not alone!
Think of all those who have been there for you.
Examples: parents, guardians, friends, siblings, a teacher, a pet.

Fill in the speech bubbles with how you can show your appreciation!

Some days you want to move forward, but you may not be able to.
There are a lot of outside influences that
we cannot control, but we can control ourselves.

Things I can control:

Things I cannot control:

You always have the option
to ask for help.

Take a breath and focus on what you can change.

Let's move **forward** together.

Don't let **anger** control you.

We all get angry from time to time.
During those moments, we must be mindful of our actions, as anger
can have destructive consequences for others and ourselves.
If you find yourself losing control, try one of these strategies.
Feel free to add your own, too!

1. Empathize with those who anger you
2. Breathe
3. Reframe the situation
4. Visualize the situation in the larger scheme of life
5. Talk it out with a friend outside of the situation
6. Take a walk
7.
8.
9.

Now, before acting, ask yourself these questions . . .

Only positive comments today!

Do I need to take action now, or can I let things be?

What would the consequences of my action/inaction be?

Will my action/inaction bring about peace, harmony, or justice?
Will it bring about pain, suffering, or despair?

What are all the possible solutions?
When you think of all of them, think of another.

Take deep breaths before acting.

Draw **what is being** juggled!

Always look **on the** bright side **of** life.

You can turn your life **around.**

Some days, it can feel like everything is going wrong.
If you're having a bad day, it's helpful to remember how strong you are.

When was a time you overcame adversity?

How did it feel afterward?

Remember that feeling!

It can be hard to smile when you're not feeling your best.
When you're having a sick day, give yourself time to heal.
Hopefully, these jokes can help you smile while you recover.
(These are my favorite!)

What is a dog's favorite dessert?
Pup-cakes!

Why did the cow cross the road?
To get to the udder side!

What is a snake's favorite subject?
Hiss-story!

Why can't a leopard hide?
Because they are always spotted!

You can **always** lean **on my** shoulders.

Let's explore this universe together.

Think **of someone** you care deeply for.
What would be the ideal vacation **for the** two **of you?**
Outline **or** doodle **it below!**

Congrats! You've made it to the end of the book.
Like beginnings, endings are great things, too.
They can sometimes be sad, but if you see life as a continuous journey,
an ending is only the start of a new adventure.
As we've come full circle, let's take a moment to reflect again.

Where do you find yourself always smiling?

What makes you smile?

When do you smile the most?

Why do you smile?

Who makes you smile?

Let's share our **joys in** life.

Every day when I publish my comic, I make sure to include a smile goal and/or question.
These goals and questions serve as prompts to help people smile.
In case you find yourself needing a smile, here are some smile goals and questions you can use when you need them.

Smile goals ⊥⊥

1. Take a walk
2. Cheer up a friend
3. Read a book
4. Donate to a charity
5. Make art
6. Pet a dog
7. Pet the dog again (it's a good boy/girl and deserves ALL the pets)
8. Let a friend know how you're doing
9. Ask a friend how they're doing
10. Ask yourself how you're doing
11. Reestablish a friendship
12. Listen to your favorite song
13. Sing a song
14. Dance a dance
15. Tell a joke
16. Help a friend
17. Help a stranger
18. Breathe
19. Take a break
20. Cook something yummy
21. Hug a friend
22. Hug yourself
23. Learn a new skill
24. Exercise
25. Meditate
26. Take time to daydream
27. Go to sleep early
28. Pay it forward
29. Get a sweet treat
30. Be in the moment

If you run out of smile goals, feel free to make your own!

Smile questions ☺

1. What is your favorite childhood memory?
2. What is your favorite dessert and why?
3. What are you most proud of?
4. What makes you happy?
5. What can you do to make others happy?
6. What would make you content?
7. Where did I put my keys? (oh, here they are)
8. What can you do to better your life?
9. What is your favorite animal and why?
10. What is your favorite dinosaur and why?
11. What is your favorite color and why?
12. How can you help the environment?
13. What small changes can you make in your life in order to improve it?
14. When was the last time you stargazed?
15. What are your goals?
16. When was the last time you took a break?
17. What is your favorite way to hug someone?
18. When was a time you were able to overcome a hardship?
19. Where is your happy place and why does it make you happy?
20. What is your vision of world peace?
21. What is your perfect day like?
22. What is your favorite way to support your loved ones?
23. What can you do to add a bit of whimsy into your life?
24. What is an act of kindess you can incorporate into your daily routine?
25. When was the last time you admired art?
26. What makes your heart fill with joy?
27. When was a time you were able to do the impossible?
28. How can you be more compassionate?
29. When was the last time you let your inner child out to play?
30. What can you do to help someone smile?

Did you know otters hold hands when they sleep?

Hidden Hearts

Beginning pages

Comic and Reflection pages

67. On the watering can
68. The leaf to the left of the parrot
69. In the third panel, the cutout on the top leaf
70. On the purple spaceship
71. On the purple spaceship
72. The falling leaf
73. One of the dirt pieces below the parrot
74. On the floorboards below the cat
75. On the puppy's cape
76. On the sweater
77. On the sweater
78. A dirt piece to the right of the mole
79. In one of the flowers
80. On the cat's paw
81. In the first panel, a cloud to the left
82. In the painting
83. In the painting
84. On the kite
85. The floating grass blades
86. In the fourth panel, above the fox's tail
87. Below the word "matter," blended in the pink background
88. The middle of the flower
89. One of the giraffe's spots
90. On the dragon's cloud
91. On the teapot
92. Blended into the purple background on the right of the page
93. Above the puppy's head
94. The water splash in the third panel
95. On the book
96. Below the word "Ikigai"
97. One of the giraffe's spots
98. One of the stars in the fourth panel
99. On the fourth earth bullet
100. A constellation above the cat
101. A continent in the third and fourth panel
102. A spot on the cow
103. Everywhere on the page
104. Blended into the blue background on the right of the page
105. On the box
106. The firefly's light
107. On the sign
108. On the squirrel's lance

109. One of the leaves in the third panel
110. Above the otter in the third panel
111. Above the rhino, blended into the teal background
112. One of the chips
113. In the painting
114. A piece of dirt in the second panel
115. All over the page
116. Blended into the yellow background on the right of the page
117. The grass blade in the third panel
118. To the left of the bear in the third panel
119. Above the laptop
120. The cutout in the chair
121. The tiny cloud above the left mountain
122. On the butterfly's wings
123. On the butterfly's wings
124. One of the cow's spots
125. On the towel
126. One of the stars in the fourth panel
127. On the mouse's dress
128. All over the page
129. On the cookie box in the fourth panel

Endpages

130. Above the fox, blended into the yellow background
131. Above the word "routine," blended into the pink background
132. Blended into the yellow background, to the right of "18. On the playing cards"
133. Blended into the pink background, to the right of this description →
134. All over the page
135. Beside the monkey
136. Beside the bunny

Acknowledgments

I would like to first thank my mom, dad, and sister for their
love and support. Without my family, I wouldn't be able to do what I do.
I love you guys from the bottom of my heart.

Thank you to all my friends at The Warren, SCBWI Midsouth,
and the Webcomic Treehouse Discord for guiding and encouraging me.

A special thank-you to Jacqueline Chen (Chibird) for
answering all my questions without hesitation.

A BIG thank-you to my agent Kathleen Ortiz and my editor Patty Rice
for believing in me and 4amShower.

Thank you to all my friends (especially my Mayfield/Suite and DFA ones)
for all the support you guys give me.

And, last but not least, thank you to all my readers and Patreon supporters
for reading my work and smiling with me. (Pst! That's YOU!)

About the Author

Guy Kopsombut is a self-taught Nashville-based artist
and creator of the daily webcomic 4amShower.
In 2015, Guy set out to help one person, any one person in the world,
smile each day with his wholesome comics.
Over the past five years, his comics have helped hundreds of
thousands of people connect, get through hard times, and smile (a lot!).

Growing up in a Buddhist household, Guy was taught how to meditate,
which he believes has given him an empathic perspective in life.
He spends his free time self-reflecting, dreaming up more
projects to help people smile, and eating yummy pastries.
When he is not drawing cute animals, Guy is
helping his parents at their Thai restaurant, The Smiling Elephant.

Instagram: 4amShower
Twitter: 4amShower
Facebook: Facebook.com/4amShower
Patreon: Patreon.com/4amShower